CHINA SINCE 1949

Simon Williams

Head of Shene School,
Richmond-on-Thames

M
MACMILLAN
EDUCATION

First published 1985
Reprinted 1986, 1987, 1988

Published by
MACMILLAN EDUCATION LTD
Houndmills, Basingstoke, Hampshire RG21 2XS
and London
Companies and representatives
throughout the world

Printed in Hong Kong

British Library Cataloguing in Publication Data
Williams, Simon
China since 1949.—(History in depth).
1. China—History—1949—
I. Title   II. Series
951.05   DS777.S5
ISBN 0–333–35199–1

Cover illustration courtesy of Chinese Visual Aids Project,
Polytechnic of Central London, School of Languages

CONTENTS

Acknowledgements

The author and publishers wish to acknowledge the following photograph sources:

Anglo Chinese Educational Institute/China Pictorial pp 19, 45 top and bottom;   Anglo Chinese Educational Institute pp 24, 25;   Camera Press pp 5, 17, 23 top left, 30, 41, 52, 53;   Chinese Visual Aids Project, Polytechnic of Central London, School of Languages pp 23 bottom, 50, 54;   John Hillelson Agency Ltd p 27;   Pictorial Press Ltd p 15;   Popperfoto pp 9, 31, 35, 48;   Frank Spooner Pictures p 38 centre; taken from Roger Garside, *Coming Alive–China Since Mao*, André Deutsch, pp 32, 38 left and right.

The author and publishers wish to thank the following who have kindly given permission for the use of copyright material:

Victor Gollancz Ltd. on behalf of Mrs Snow for an extract from *The Other Side of the River* by the late Edgar Snow; Hodder & Stoughton Ltd. for an extract from *China: Alive in the Bitter Sea* by Fox Butterfield; Monthly Review Press for an extract from *Fanshen: A Documentary of Revolution in a Chinese Village* by William Hinton, copyright © 1966 by William Hinton; *The Observer* newspaper for an extract from an article by Jonathan Mirsky; Oxford University Press for an extract from *Origins of the Cultural Revolution*, Vol. 2, 1983, by Roderick MacFarquhar.

The publishers have made every effort to trace the copyright holders, but where they have failed to do so they will be pleased to make the necessary arrangements at the first opportunity.

PREFACE

The study of history is exciting, whether in a good story well told, a mystery solved by the judicious unravelling of clues, or a study of the men, women and children whose fears and ambitions, successes and tragedies make up the collective memory of mankind.

This series aims to reveal this excitement to pupils through a set of topic books on important historical subjects from the Middle Ages to the present day. Each book contains four main elements: a narrative and descriptive text, lively and relevant illustrations, extracts of contemporary evidence, and questions for further thought and work. Involvement in these elements should provide an adventure which will bring the past to life in the imagination of the pupil.

Each book is also designed to develop the knowledge, skills and concepts so essential to a pupil's growth. It provides a wide, varying introduction to the evidence available on each topic. In handling this evidence, pupils will increase their understanding of basic historical concepts such as causation and change, as well as of more advanced ideas such as revolution and democracy. In addition, their use of basic study skills will be complemented by more sophisticated historical skills such as the detection of bias and the formulation of opinion.

The intended audience for the series is pupils of eleven to sixteen years: it is expected that the earlier topics will be introduced in the first three years of secondary school, while the nineteenth and twentieth century topics are directed towards first examinations.

Chinese names

This book uses the newer pinyin system for spelling names. With pinyin the name is spelt more or less as it is pronounced in Chinese. Examples of names which appear in the book are given below with both their old and new spelling.

OLD	NEW (pinyin)
Mao Tse-tung	Mao Zedong
Cho En-lai	Zhou Enlai
Chiang Ch'ing	Jiang Qing
Teng Hsiao-p'ing	Deng Xiaoping
Peking	Beijing
Canton	Guangdong
Yangtse	Changjiang
Kuomintan	Guomindang

THE EARLY YEARS OF COMMUNIST RULE

The challenge

On 1 October 1949, Mao Zedong stood on the high rostrum of the Gate of Heavenly Peace in Beijing and announced to the packed square below that the new People's Republic of China had been formed. It was a triumphant moment for the Communist Party. After years of fighting against their political opponents, the Guomindang, the Communists had finally won the struggle to control China. The Guomindang survivors, led by Chiang Kai-shek, had fled for safety to the nearby island of Taiwan.

Right: *China and its neighbours*

Below: *Mao announces the new Republic of China*

China and its neighbours map showing:

USSR

MONGOLIA

CHINA

NEPAL

INDIA

BURMA

THAILAND

NORTH VIETNAM

LAOS

NORTH KOREA

SOUTH KOREA

JAPAN

TAIWAN

Beijing

Shanghai

Guangzhou

River Changjiang

- - - - Route of Long March, 1934-5

Mainland areas of China occupied by Japan in 1944

Victory was particularly sweet for Mao Zedong. The son of a peasant, Mao was one of the 12 delegates who had founded the Chinese Communist Party in 1921. He became its leader during the Long March of 1934–5, at a time when the party's position was desperate. The Communists were on the run from the pursuing armies of the Guomindang and in danger of being completely wiped out. Mao led them to safety in northern China where they began to build up their support amongst the peasants. They taught them to read and write and they gave them their own land to farm which they had seized from the landlords.

In 1937 Mao Zedong was faced with a different enemy when Japanese forces invaded China. The Communist Red Army led the national struggle against the brutal Japanese occupation and by the time Japan withdrew from China after their defeat in World War II the Communists controlled much of northern China. A year later, in 1946, civil war broke out again between the Communists and the Guomindang, but now the Communists had the upper hand. While Chiang Kai-shek raged against his generals, his armies deserted to the enemy. By 1949 the Communists had won a popular victory and it had been masterminded by the shrewd and determined Mao.

The new Communist leaders of China needed all the support they could get. Beyond the cheering crowds in Beijing lay a nation ravaged by years of war and famine. The Communists had to govern a vast country (nearly 50 times the size of Britain) with a population of more than 500 million. Ninety per cent of the people were peasants and most of them lived a back-breaking life of poverty at the mercy of both the landlords and the weather. Foreign businessmen owned most of the little industry there was in China. In the cities prices had risen by 25 per cent each week in the last few months of the civil war. People exchanged goods as money became worthless. Criminal gangs flourished on the profits of the opium trade while beggars died on the streets through lack of food.

The Communists set to work with speed and ruthless efficiency. In 1952, a foreign visitor to the city of Guangzhou remarked:

Prostitution, opium addiction, gambling and alcoholism were virtually wiped out . . . for the first time for a century people did not have to worry about robbery or walking the street alone in the evening.

China's industry

Mao was determined to build up China's industry as quickly as possible. The country had to produce far more coal, iron and steel if it was to escape from poverty and defend itself from outside attack. China turned to its Communist neighbour, the Soviet Union, for help. In 1950 the Soviet Union agreed to build three hundred modern industrial plants in China over the next 15 years. Most of China's own money was spent on constructing huge iron and steel works and

China's first mass-produced lorries

equipping the factories that would produce industrial goods such as motor vehicles and aircraft. The Communist Party followed the example of the Soviet Union and took control of all industry in China. The Five Year Plan, started in 1953, stated exactly how much would be spent and how much should be produced by each industry and each factory. A visitor to north-eastern China described the new scene as a 'lunar landscape of new bricks and drifting smoke, heavily guarded bridges, great gangs and communities of people laying immense girders over river beds'. By 1957 coal production had doubled and four times as much steel was being produced as in 1952.

Revolution in the countryside

During the civil war most landlords had supported the Guomindang, while most peasants had supported the Communists. One of Mao's first tasks was to take away the power which the landlords had exercised over the peasants for hundreds of years.

'A revolution,' said Mao, 'is not the same as inviting people to dinner.... It is an act of violence whereby one class overthrows another.' The revolution that Mao carried out in the villages of China was certainly no dinner party. By 1952 between two and three million landlords had been killed. What this revolution meant to those involved has been vividly described by an American writer who spent

7

six months in the village of Longbow immediately after the Communists had taken over the village from the Japanese in 1945. The Communists persuaded the peasants to start a campaign against the landlords. Several were beaten to death and others were driven out of the village. All their land and possessions were divided up and handed out to the peasants. Within a few months the world of the people of Longbow had been turned upside down.

Using the evidence: the revolution in Longbow

Peasants' Association: peasant organisation set up by the Communists to carry out land reform

cadres: (in this context) Communist officials

militiaman: soldier

A The Committee of the Peasants' Association decided to tackle Kuo Ch'ung-wang first. He was not the richest man in the village but he was one of the meanest . . . while his tenants died of starvation during the famine years, he seized grain and hoarded it for speculation. The cadres . . . held small group meetings ahead of time in order to gather opinions against Ch'ung-wang. Those with serious grievances were encouraged to make them known amongst their closest neighbours and were then mobilised to speak out at the village-wide meetings.

On the day of the big meeting, the grain which could have saved the lives of dozens of people lay in the courtyard in a stinking mildewed heap. . . . At this critical meeting, Fu-yuan, the village head, was the first to speak . . . 'In the famine year . . . my brother worked for your family. We were all hungry. We had nothing to eat. But you had no thought for us. Several times we tried to borrow grain from you. But it was all in vain. You watched us starve without pity.'

Then Ho-pang, a militiaman, spoke up. His voice shook as he told how he had rented land from Ch'ung-wang. 'One year I could not pay the rent. You took the whole harvest. You took my clothes. You took everything.' He broke down sobbing as a dozen others jumped up shouting, 'Speak'.

'Yes, speak. Make him talk. Let's hear his answers.' But Ch'ung-wang had no answers. He could not utter a word.

The next morning when the people met again to carry on the campaign against Ch'ung-wang, excitement ran high. Women even went so far as to bring food with them so that they and their families could stay right through the day and not miss a single minute. Liang, the district leader, opened the attack. . . . 'Even if you take all his property it will never be enough. Ask him where he has hidden all his gold and silver.'

'Yes, speak out. Where are the coins? Where have you buried the money?' came the shouts from the crowd. But Ch'ung-wang refused to say anything beyond the fact that he had no silver and never had any. . . . *The militia were ordered into his house to make a search . . . they found nothing. . . . After several people had talked to him, Ch'ung-wang finally gave in. He told them where to dig. They found fifty silver dollars in an earthen crock.*

When this money was brought before the people at the meeting, they became very angry. Here was proof that Ch'ung-wang had lied to them. Scores of people jumped up, ran forward, and began to beat him with whatever came to hand.

'Tell us where the rest is. You know that is not all,' they shouted. Someone struck him a blow in the face. Ch'ung-wang held his bleeding mouth and tried to speak.

'Don't hit me. I'll tell you right away. There is another 80 dollars in the back room.' That day he gave up more than 200 silver dollars.'

The following day Ch'ung-wang and his wife ran away. His brother and business partner was brought before the Peasants' Association and beaten so severely that he died.

William Hinton: *Fanshen*, 1966

B   *The fate of a landlord in another village*

C Ownership of land in Longbow before and after Land Reform

1944

Group	Number of people	% of population	% of land held
Landlord/rich peasant	63	7	31
Less prosperous peasant	395	40	45
Poor peasant	462	47	24
Hired labourer	59	6	0

1948

Group	Number of people	% of population	% of land held
Landlord/rich peasant	14	1.5	1.2
Less prosperous peasant	864	90	90.8
Poor peasant	82	8.5	7.4

William Hinton: *Fanshen*, 1966

D Two peasants from Longbow describe how their lives have changed:

Shen Fa-liang, the former hired labourer, said, 'Life is much better than before. Now I have land and a house and work to do. There is grain in my house. I work very hard but I enjoy the results of my work because I carry all the results of my work back home and put it in my own jars. But in the past it was just the opposite. I laboured very hard regardless of rain or shine but all that work was for others not for me. All the crops were very beautiful but all the crops I had to carry to someone else's granary. Now I work for myself.'

Chung-lai's wife felt the same way. 'In the old days I worked as a servant. I was busy every night until midnight, and I had to get up before dawn. Now I am very busy too but now I work for myself. This is happy labour. . . . My condition now is good. I've got a house, land to till, clothes to wear and the right to speak. Who dared speak before? In the past when I served in other families, even when they didn't beat or curse me, still, if I committed some trifling offence their eyebrows and their eyes met. It is hard to eat with another's bowl. To live in one's own house and eat out of one's own bowl is the happiest life.'

William Hinton: *Fanshen*, 1966

Questions

1   According to source **A** what action did the cadres take against Ch'ung-wang? Why do you think they didn't leave the Peasants' Association to organise the trial?

2   In every village in China, the Communists involved the peasants directly in the campaign against the landlords.
    a)   Why do you think that the Communists insisted on involving the peasants?
    b)   In what ways were the peasants in source **A** directly involved in the trial of Ch'ung-wang?
    c)   Bearing in mind Mao's view that the landlords were the enemies of the people, how else might the Communists have dealt with the landlords? What would have been the advantages and disadvantages of a different approach?

3   Imagine that Ch'ung-wang was discovered and brought back to face his accusers. You are the leader of the Peasants' Association. Write the speech that you would have given in the courtyard in which you:
    a)   sum up the charges against Ch'ung-wang
    b)   explain why the peasants are so bitter towards him
    c)   pronounce sentence upon him.

4   Source **B** shows the trial of a different landlord in another village. What appears to be a) similar b) different between this trial and the trial of Ch'ung-wang in Longbow?

5   Use document **C** to draw a bar chart comparing the percentage of land owned by different groups of the population in 1944 and 1948. What are the main changes that have taken place?

6   Make a list of all the ways in which life had improved for each of the two peasants in source **D**. What things did they both agree had improved? In what single respect had both their lives remained the same?

The move to co-operative farms

The dream of peasants across the world is to own the land they farm. In Longbow, as in the other villages of China, the dream came true. But it did not last. By 1957 all the peasants in China had handed over their land to the State and were working on large co-operative farms. In a Communist society, this change was hardly surprising. Communists believe that where individuals are allowed to own 'the means of production', whether it is land or factories, the people become divided into the 'haves' and the 'have nots'. Even if all the peasants started by owning roughly the same amount of land, it would not be long before some peasants bought land from others. The richer peasants would soon become landlords and the poorer peasants would become hired labourers.

Another important reason for the move to co-operative farming was that the Communist Party had to find ways of producing more food for the rapidly increasing population. Since coming to power the Communists had quickly provided simple but effective medical care and, as a result, the death rate dropped dramatically. In 1949, out of every thousand babies born, 140 died before the age of one. By 1956 that figure had dropped to 37. This dramatic improvement meant that every year there were more than two million extra mouths to feed. Yet only a tenth of China's land could produce food as most of the remainder was mountain or desert. That meant that the land already being farmed had to be farmed more efficiently.

The land which the peasants had been given was insufficient to produce the extra food. In Longbow, for example, most peasants had less than an acre of land. If the peasants worked together on larger areas of land, they could share labour, tools and animals. They could also build the canals and reservoirs that were needed to prevent the frequent floods and droughts from destroying the crops.

As the table on page 13 shows, the Communists organised the move to co-operative farms in stages. First the peasants formed small mutual-aid teams and worked together on each other's land. Then they joined lower stage co-operatives where they handed over their land to the co-operative and were paid according to how much they had owned and how much work they did. Finally, they formed higher stage co-operatives. These were much bigger, consisting of about three hundred families, and the peasants were paid only according to how much work they did. In the Soviet Union, 20 years earlier, the peasants had burnt their crops and slaughtered their own animals when they were forced to hand their land over to the State. Yet this did not happen in China. Why were the peasants apparently willing to hand over their new land to the State?

Using the evidence

A *Our first year as a [lower stage co-operative] was very tough. Floods destroyed both our spring and summer crops, except on one farm, and by August we had nothing to eat. . . . We called a meeting and persuaded the one family with a surplus to lend the co-op seed and food instead of selling at a good profit. We had enough food to eat for one month.*

Very late in the season, then, we eight families, adults and children all working, planted our land in vegetables for one more try. Other peasants laughed at us; they thought we would never be able to bring in our crop. By intensive cultivation, luck and shock-brigade methods we brought in a rich harvest in record time. That year our income increased by more than half. We were able to buy not only tools and seeds but eight bales of cloth to make winter clothes for our family . . . seven of those families had never before owned a new suit of clothes.

After our success . . . more than fifty families asked to join. . . . In 1955 we took in another village and had altogether 296 families. We formed an advanced co-operative . . . we were able to organise labour more efficiently, to build roads, dikes and canals and to dig wells.
    The Chairman of one co-operative farm, quoted in Edgar
    Snow's book, *The Other Side of the River*, 1963

B *Percentage of families in China in different types of co-operative farms*

Year	Mutual aid	Lower co-operatives	Advanced co-operatives
1953	39.3	0.2	—
1954	58.3	1.9	—
1955	32.7	63.3	4.0
1956	3.7	8.5	87.8
1957	—	—	93.5

C *Grain production and population figures in China*

Item	1949	1952	1957
Grain (millions of tons)	111	161	191
Population (millions)	542	575	646

Questions

1 Why, according to source **A**, was the lower stage co-operative on the edge of disaster? What action did its members take which prevented disaster?

2 Why do you think that families asked to join the co-operative?

3 Why is it necessary to have additional evidence to that provided by source **A** before the historian can be sure that this is an accurate account of what happened both in this village and in other Chinese villages? What sort of evidence would the historian look for?

4 Why do you think that the Communists carried out the move to co-operative farms in stages instead of bringing in advanced co-operative farms straight away?

5 Use the evidence in all three sources to say whether the move to co-operative farming was successful or not.

The Communist achievement

By 1957, the Communists had turned China into a very different country from the one they had taken over in 1949. For the first time for more than a hundred years there was a strong government in control. The Communist Party had developed China's industries and built up its defences. It had pushed through a revolution in the countryside by getting rid of the landlords and winning peasant support for co-operative farms. Most Chinese people were better off under the Communists. People had more food to eat and they could expect to live longer. Whereas in 1949 85 per cent of the population was illiterate, by 1957 most Chinese could read and write. Women, in particular, had benefited from Communist rule. In old China women were expected to look after the house, rear sons and obey their husbands. In 1950 the Communists declared that 'women enjoy equal rights with men'. Girls now went to school and women were encouraged to go out to work. The practice of killing unwanted baby girls was officially abolished (although it still continues, see Chapter 6) and for the first time women were allowed to divorce their husbands.

2 THE GREAT LEAP FORWARD

China in 1958 was a scene of frenzied activity. Across the country peasants marched out to work singing revolutionary songs. Using spades and shovels, they dug up earth to make dams, canals and reservoirs. Newspapers carried reports of people working, eating and sleeping in the fields day and night. Slogans were painted on village houses and carved onto hillside rocks:

Produce more, faster, better. Three Years of Bitter Struggle. Ten Thousand Years of Joy.

Mao had launched the Great Leap Forward. The aim was for China to catch up with Britain in 15 years. By then, steel production would have risen from 5 to 40 million tons a year. One factory worker described what happened:

We were told that China would get rich quick if everyone concentrated on iron and steel. So we dropped everything else and built brick chimneys in the factory yards. Radiators, pots and pans . . . went into ovens and peasants poured in from the countryside to help.

Peasants marching out to work

In the villages peasants made their own iron from backyard blast-furnaces. Children in Shanghai made bricks out of earth and water in their lessons. Older students stayed up all night making steel or smashing earth and stones to make concrete.

Why did Mao launch the Great Leap Forward?

At 65 years of age, Mao Zedong was a leader in a hurry. He was determined to turn China into a powerful industrial nation as quickly as possible. Much had already been achieved. But, for Mao, the pace was too slow and the money needed to set up the big factories was scarce. If China was short of money, it was not short of people. Why build expensive steel mills when the peasants could produce steel in their own backyards? Why not use the muscle power of the peasants to stop the frequent floods and droughts that threatened the country with mass starvation? Under Mao's new plan peasants would no longer drift to the cities in search of work that was not available. Instead, each area of the country would produce its own food, develop its own industries, train its own soldiers and provide work for all its people.

The communes

To create this new China, Mao set up communes across the country. Several co-operative farms and villages were joined together to form one commune. 30 000 people on average belonged to each commune. It looked after the needs of all its members from the cradle to the grave: health clinics, schools, open-air cinemas and 'Happiness Homes' for the elderly were all provided. Mothers put their babies into the nurseries and went out to work in the fields. Each commune had its factories and workshops, where farm tools were made and crops from the land were processed. With so many people under their control, the commune leaders were able to organise the peasants to build roads and construct dams and reservoirs.

In the co-operative farms peasants had kept their own small plot of land on which they grew vegetables and reared pigs. They now handed these plots over to the commune. In some communes the peasants handed over everything they owned: beds, furniture, bicycles, pots and pans. They left their houses to live in 'communal habitation centres' where they slept in unisex dormitories and ate all their meals in nearby canteens. To Mao and his supporters the communes were a short-cut to the true Communist society. When people no longer owned and fought over possessions and property, they would work for the good of all and not for themselves.

Disaster

In 1958 the *People's Daily* newspaper announced that 'today, in the era of Mao Zedong, Heaven is here on earth'. But for many Chinese the next few years were more like hell on earth. According to one estimate, 20 million people died of starvation or related diseases

16

Commune members building a new canal

between 1959 and 1962. What had gone wrong with Mao's bold experiment?

A series of natural disasters badly affected the harvests. In 1960, north and central China had their worst drought for a hundred years. The Yellow River, which irrigates half the cultivated land in the country, almost completely dried up. Further south there was serious and widespread flooding.

In the same year as the drought and floods, the Soviet Union suddenly ordered all its scientists and engineers working in China to return home. Nikita Khrushchev, the Soviet leader, strongly disapproved of what Mao was doing. The communes, he said, had been tried before in the Soviet Union and failed. He called the Great Leap Forward 'a dangerous experiment' that could only lead to disaster. The Soviet scientists returned to Moscow with their factory plans in their suitcases. As a result, factories under construction could not be finished and some factories already built had to be closed down as the supply of spare parts from the Soviet Union dried up.

However, the Great Leap Forward had already started to go badly wrong before 1960. The main responsibility for the disaster rested with Mao. Although it made sense to bring more work to the countryside in order to stop the peasants leaving the land, Mao was in too much of a hurry and he did not give enough thought to the practical problems that would be created by the Great Leap Forward. The documents below illustrate what these problems were. They also shed some light on the attitude of the peasants. If there was so much suffering, why didn't the peasants openly rebel against the government?

Using the evidence: what went wrong?

A 'But where are those five hundred million peasants?' my Soviet colleague wondered. 'Why are they not in the fields? It's the spring planting season, isn't it?' The answer to that query could be found in the thousands of smoking chimneys we saw each day, and in the fires that were visible every night over the horizon. The peasants were carrying out the orders of the Party, working night and day at the mines and home-made blast furnaces to fulfil the 'Drive to Produce Metals Locally'. And we know the results: they did not obtain any more iron than before, and there was much less bread and rice to go round. . . .

According to the official figure, 4 million tons of iron were processed, but of this amount hardly more than one per cent was usable, the remaining 99 per cent being slag, unwashed ore, or even more often, a pure invention of the statisticians.

Mikhail Klochko: *Soviet Scientist in China*, 1964

B *Production figures (in millions of tons)*

	1957	1960
Grain	195.05	143.5
Steel	5.35	18
Coal	130	390

Grain ration (kilograms per person)

1957	203	1960	163.5

P'eng: at the time of his visit to this commune, P'eng Teh-huai was Minister of Defence. What he saw on his visit convinced him that China was facing a disaster. When he spoke out against Mao and the Great Leap Forward in 1959, he was sacked

C *P'eng came upon a large pile of ripe crops lying on the ground apparently abandoned.*

After a lengthy search, an old peasant was finally located who explained that all the able-bodied people were busy launching a steel sputnik (i.e. attempting to set a record in steel production).

P'eng exclaimed: 'Hasn't any one of you given a thought to what you will eat next year if you don't bring in the crops? You're never going to be able to eat steel.' The old peasant nodded vigorously in agreement, but added pointedly, 'True enough. Who would disagree with that. But who can stand up against the wind?'

Roderick MacFarquhar: *Origins of the Cultural Revolution*, volume 2, 1983

D *Peasants working through the night*

China Pictorial, 1958

E *A meal is brought to the workers in the fields*

China Pictorial, 1958

F *All property has to be state-owned, all houses and furniture have been turned into government property. They do what they like. No one has any right at all.*

People fight each other to get to the rice barrels first, but there is never enough.

Nor are there vegetables available, not to mention fish and meat. Only sick people with certificates are permitted to buy.

*There is nothing for sale; there is nothing to eat when we are
hungry. People are afraid to die because they feel they will
be unable to close their eyes when they are dead. . . .
Everybody is suffering. Everything is gone.*
Extracts from letters sent by peasants to relatives living
outside China, 1958—9.

Roderick MacFarquhar: *Origins of the Cultural Revolution*,
volume 2, 1983

G *In the spring of 1960, the peasants were given production
targets they considered quite impossible to meet. That year
there were appalling natural disasters. Passive resistance
grew. The harvest was late. For the second time deliveries of
food to the State had to be extracted by force from a hungry
peasant population.*

Sven Lindquist: *China in Crisis*, 1963

Questions
1   Select from the different sources above all the main evidence
    which shows that food production fell during the Great Leap
    Forward.
2   Which source suggests that food production was rising? Why
    do you think there is a difference of view over whether food
    production was rising or falling? Which view do you accept and
    why?
3   What is the main reason put forward in sources **A** and **C** to
    explain why food production fell?
4   Which two sources suggest that Mao's plan to increase iron
    and steel production was successful? What evidence can you
    find from the other sources which disagrees with this view?
    Which view do you agree with and why?
5   a)   According to source **G** what did the peasants do or not do
         when faced with famine?
    b)   What did the old peasant mean in source **C** when he said
         'who can stand up against the wind'?
    c)   How does source **F** help to explain why the peasants didn't
         actively protest against the government?
6   Imagine you are a peasant living in 1960 in a commune whose
    members are faced with famine. Write a letter to a relative living
    abroad referring to the following points:
    a)   how your village became part of a commune
    b)   the new work you had to do after the Great Leap Forward
         had been launched
    c)   how famine came to your village
    d)   your thoughts and feelings about what you have been
         through in the last two years.

3

THE CULTURAL REVOLUTION

Communism in danger!

In 1966 Mao Zedong summoned the young people of China to the same central square in Beijing where 17 years earlier he had announced the Communist victory in the civil war. Now his message was different: the Communist revolution was in danger, not from enemies outside China, but from some of the leaders of the Communist Party itself. The young people, who became known as the Red Guards, were told that their task was to save the revolution. As they left Beijing to carry out their orders, it became clear that Mao Zedong had declared war on his own party.

After the Great Leap

Senior Communists had privately blamed Mao for the disastrous failure of the Great Leap Forward. He remained Chairman of the party but resigned as Head of State in 1959 and effective control over China's affairs passed to two veterans of the civil war, Liu Shaoqi and Deng Xiaoping. Determined to get the economy moving again, they gave back to the peasants their small private plots of land which they could farm after they had worked on the commune. Once again the peasants cycled into the country markets to sell their own vegetables and animals. The communes remained, although reduced in size, but the communal dormitories were abandoned and the backyard steel furnaces grew rusty with neglect. Workers were paid, partly at least, according to how hard they worked and how much they produced.

In Mao's view, these changes were turning China into a sick and selfish society where people were more concerned about themselves than their neighbours. The peasants were working harder on their own land than they were on the communes. In the cities, the young were more interested in following the latest foreign fashions in clothes and pop music than in studying how they could become good Communists.

Communist Party officials were the worst offenders in Mao's eyes. Instead of setting an example by serving the people, they were using their power for their own ends: obtaining seaside holidays, extra rations of food and clothing and bigger flats for their families to live in.

Mao's comeback

Mao withdrew to his mountain retreat to plan his next move. It was no use arguing with the new leaders, but he was convinced that the Chinese people would listen to him. He told a foreign journalist that 'the masses and I are alone'. Indeed, Mao still enjoyed tremendous prestige and authority in the country as the man who had defeated the Japanese and crushed the landlords.

Mao decided that China needed a new revolution which would get rid of all those responsible for leading the country away from the correct path to Communism. He turned to the young people to act as his troops. They were China's future and they needed the experience of revolution which Mao's generation had gained during the civil war.

In 1966 Mao announced his return to public life with a 15-kilometre swim in the Changjiang river in front of a large and enthusiastic crowd and shortly afterwards he launched the Cultural Revolution. All secondary schools and universities were closed and millions of young people poured into Beijing from all over the country travelling on free rail passes. At the huge rallies attended by Mao, they were given their orders: 'Smash the old world and bring in the new.'

'Smashing the old world'

The Red Guards enthusiastically set about their task of 'smashing the old world'. They took over the streets, banging gongs and shouting slogans. They ransacked churches and temples, tore down shop signs and invaded people's houses. They destroyed books, photographs, antiques and records – anything, in fact, that did not put over the message of Mao's Communism. People who followed fashion hurriedly cut their hair, wriggled out of their tight trousers or threw away their jewellery. Everyone, men and women alike, now wore the standard uniform of the new China, tunics and baggy trousers.

Attacking the enemy

Jiang Qing: a former actress, married Mao during the civil war. She played no part in Chinese politics until the 1960s, when she became one of the leading supporters of the Cultural Revolution

Urged on by Mao's wife, Jiang Qing, the Red Guards turned their attention to what she called the 'black dogs, slippery backsliders and rotten eggs' within the Communist Party. Their main target was Liu Shaoqi, who had taken over from Mao as Head of State. Accusing him of being the 'No. 1 Enemy of Communism', the Red Guards broke into Liu's house, physically attacked him and forced him to write his own confession. Eventually, in 1969, he was expelled from the party and died shortly afterwards as a result of being refused proper medical treatment for diabetes and pneumonia. By then the Red Guards had attacked hundreds of thousands of other party officials. Many died as a result of their treatment; others committed suicide. It was not only Communist Party members who suffered at the hands of the Red Guards. Anybody who was in a position of authority, such as school teachers, doctors and factory managers, risked being branded by the Red Guards as enemies of the Cultural Revolution. Artists and musicians who had been influenced by foreign ideas were singled out for particularly vicious treatment by Jiang Qing. One famous Com-

Right: *Party officials in disgrace. What do you think is happening to them?*

Above: *Liu Shaoqi. At the time of this photograph he was still in office but under attack from the Red Guards*

Right: *Poster showing a worker crushing Deng Xiaoping and Liu Shaoqi*

munist writer, Ding Ling, was sent to a remote village in the far north of China where she was made to do heavy manual work. The Red Guards kicked and punched her at 'struggle sessions' to make her confess to her 'crimes' and she was then forced to sleep in a cowshed.

'Bringing in the new world'

While the Red Guards were attacking the 'enemies' of Communism they were also attempting to build Mao's new China. The plan for the new society was contained in one small book, *The Thoughts of Chairman Mao*. Virtually nothing else was printed in China for two years, as millions of copies rolled off the printing presses. Its basic message was simple: work hard, follow the teachings of Chairman Mao and all problems can be solved.

Carrying their sleeping bags and copies of the 'little red book', the Red Guards travelled across China spreading the message of the Cultural Revolution. An English teacher working in China noted:

The Red Guards have changed the face of the countryside, whitewashing the houses and helping to paint slogans on the walls, such as 'Long Live Chairman Mao'. The students also stop on the way to help on the land; we saw them working in the fields or sitting in groups with the villagers, deep in study with their red book of quotations.

Red Guards and peasants studying The Thoughts of Chairman Mao *in the fields*

The new Emperor

As the Cultural Revolution got under way, China seemed to be in the grip of a new and powerful religion. At the centre was the god-like figure of Mao himself. For three thousand years the Chinese had worshipped the Emperor as the Son of Heaven and now it seemed as though Mao was the new Emperor. In the junior schools children sang:

Father is dear, Mother is dear,
But Chairman Mao is dearest of all.

Peasants and factory workers gathered together before work in front of a portrait of Chairman Mao and read passages from the 'little red book'. In the evening, they reported on the day's work, describing all the things they had done to help build the new China as well as confessing any mistakes they had made. The meeting closed with everybody saying 'May the Chairman live ten thousand years'.

Railway staff and passengers studying the 'little red book' on a train

Everywhere in China there were statues and portraits of Chairman Mao and the loudspeakers blared out the songs of the Cultural Revolution:

Chairman Mao loves the people.
He is our Guide.
He leads us onward
To build a new China.

The end of the Red Guards

For two years the Red Guards carried out Mao's orders. Then in July 1968 he summoned their leaders to his residence in Beijing, where he told them 'You have let me down'. Shortly afterwards, the army broke up the Red Guards and millions of students were forced to leave the cities and go and work in the countryside. Mao had turned on his young supporters in order to bring the country under control. Earlier he had admitted, after touring the provinces, that China was in a state of civil war. Widespread fighting had broken out as party officials under attack from the Red Guards put together their own armies to do battle with them. The Red Guards had made the situation worse by forming rival groups, each claiming to be more loyal to Mao than the others. According to one report of events in Guangxi province, in the south of China:

Hundreds, even thousands of rival red revolutionaries, fight it out with everything from bottles and bicycle chains to modern automatic weapons seized from the soldiers....

Mao in control
Mao did not view this chaos as a defeat. The Red Guards had served his purpose by driving his opponents out of office. He and his supporters had forced their way back to the centre of the political stage where they remained until his death in 1976. They were now in a position to take China back on what they considered to be the proper path towards a true Communist society.

The government stopped bonuses for extra work in the factories and paid the workers equal wages. They took away the private plots of land from the peasants and only allowed them one fruit tree outside their house, four chickens and one pig. They closed down the country markets along with thousands of family shops and restaurants.

Jiang Qing and her supporters controlled what people did in their spare time. They ordered people to stop playing chess, collecting stamps and keeping pets because they took their minds away from politics. They stopped the popular Saturday night dances and the stand-up comedians were no longer allowed to perform their acts. All books, operas, plays and films had to praise Mao and attack the enemies of the Cultural Revolution.

China's leaders virtually sealed China off from the rest of the world. Hardly any Chinese were allowed to study at universities abroad. The few foreigners who were allowed to live in China had no contact with the ordinary Chinese people, who were forbidden to speak to them. One rare visitor reported that no one would even point him the way when he was lost in the middle of a busy city.

When the students finally returned to their schools and universities, they found that much had changed there. From the time of his own childhood, Mao had distrusted teachers and education. He told his own daughter to go and tell the poor peasants: 'Papa says that after studying a few years we become more and more stupid. Please be my teachers. I want to learn from you.' Students of all ages were now made to learn from the peasants and factory workers by spending part of their education working in farms or factories. Mao also abolished examinations on the grounds that they were unfair to the poorer workers. University places went to students who supported the Cultural Revolution and came from a humble background.

School children building a pavement

Using the evidence: one girl's story

It has been estimated that 400 000 people were killed during the Cultural Revolution. The lives of many more were ruined by the actions of the Red Guards. One such person was Lihua, who was six years old when her father was arrested in 1966. The Red Guards had found out that he had been a member of the Guomindang for a short while. In this interview with a foreign journalist, which took place in Beijing in the early 1980s, Lihua described what happened next:

'Red Guards came to search our house, they confiscated everything. They took my father's books, my mother's jewellery, her college photo albums, everything. That was the end of my childhood.'

Afterwards, the Public Security Bureau ordered her entire family to move to a village eight hundred miles south of Peking. . . . Six teenage Red Guards accompanied the family on the three-day train trip to make sure they got there.

'When we arrived, the local cadres took away the few things we had left, our clothes and our bedding. They left us only what we had on our backs.' The family was put in the village schoolhouse, a small one-room building with holes in the wall where the windows should have been and a roof that leaked. There was no furniture.

'The peasants and cadres made my parents parade through the streets every day for several weeks,' she related. 'They hung a placard round my father's neck, they made him kneel down to confess his crimes and they beat both my father and mother with iron bars.' . . . Within a month her mother was dead and her father was left deaf and unable to use his right arm. . . .

After [that] she had to find a way to earn a living for the cadres at first wouldn't let her brothers take part in working in the collective fields. The one thing she found she could do as a six-year-old was to go out to the mountains to collect firewood to sell to a brick-kiln nearby.

'I would walk ten miles up to the hills at sunrise every day, then back that evening. Sometimes I had to carry a hundred pounds, almost twice my weight. . . . In that first year, our clothes soon became like tattered pieces of paper. I had to teach myself how to sew for the family by taking apart our old clothes and then putting them back together.

'We had to borrow or beg a few ounces of rice or sweet potatoes from the other peasants. . . . Sometimes we were so short of food we had to eat the husks of the rice too. I would make them into pancakes. But they were so hard that I couldn't swallow them unless I was very hungry.

'I want people outside China to know what the Cultural Revolution was like and what the Chinese have been through. . . . I won't be happy till I die. I've never lived a good day in my life. My mother was beaten to death, my father was left senseless. That is what the Cultural Revolution did. It is unfixable. My scars will never heal.'

Fox Butterfield: *China*, 1982

Questions

1 Lihua's father was arrested because he had been a member of the Guomindang for a short while before 1949. Why was this a crime in the eyes of the Red Guards?

2 How can you tell from this passage that:
   a) the Red Guards were very powerful in China at the time of Lihua's arrest?
   b) they were no longer powerful when she spoke to the journalist about her experiences?

3 What evidence is there in this passage that:
   a) the peasants treated Lihua's family harshly?
   b) the family received some help from the peasants?
   What reasons can you think of to explain this difference in the way the peasants treated her family?

4 a) Why did Lihua want to tell her story to a foreign journalist?
   b) Why is it useful to have the sort of evidence that Lihua provides when studying the Cultural Revolution?
   c) Does Lihua's account provide a complete picture of the activities of the Red Guards during the Cultural Revolution? Explain your answer.

4 MAO AND AFTER

Gang of Four: the four leading supporters of the Cultural Revolution. One of the four was Mao's wife, Jiang Qing

By the 1970s Mao's supporters, led by the 'Gang of Four', had become increasingly concerned about one particular question: would they, and the new China of the Cultural Revolution, survive Mao's death? The Gang of Four was unpopular. People's living standards had not improved and their lives had become much duller as a result of the Cultural Revolution. Millions of Chinese people felt bitter about what had happened to them and their families. Alongside those who had suffered at the hands of the Red Guards were the former Red Guards themselves. They were still living in exile in the countryside, forbidden to return to their homes and families.

Mao himself was having doubts about whether the Gang of Four should take over from him. Towards the end of his life he was no longer on speaking terms with his wife. He thought she had become arrogant and told her so: 'You always blame others. You never blame yourself.' Mao even took the step of bringing back Deng Xiaoping to office. Together with Liu Shaoqi, Deng had taken over from Mao after the Great Leap Forward. He had been one of the main targets of the Red Guards and had spent much of the Cultural Revolution in disgrace working as a labourer. Now in 1973 Mao brought him back as Deputy Premier. With Deng back in favour and Mao increasingly frail, the fate of the Cultural Revolution and the future of China hung in the balance.

Deng Xiaoping

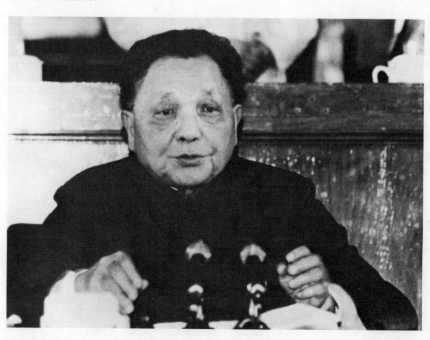

30

The April demonstrations

In 1976 popular feeling against the Gang of Four spilled into the open when Beijing's central square became the scene of mass demonstrations and riots. In January, the much-respected Zhou Enlai, Premier of China since 1949, died of cancer. During the Cultural Revolution Zhou had tried to restrain the Red Guards and it was widely known in China that he was opposed to the Gang of Four. In April, at the traditional Festival of the Dead, hundreds of thousands of people poured into the square to pay their respects to Zhou. They laid wreaths and recited poems in his memory. Some went further and wrote poems attacking the Gang of Four.

The Gang of Four, with Mao's support, took action against the demonstrators. In the early hours of 5 April they sent in two hundred trucks to remove the wreaths. During the day huge crowds filled the square and a few of the protesters set fire to some army trucks and the army command post. Most of the crowd went home after the mayor made an appeal, but a few thousand people remained. At 9.35 p.m. the lights were switched on and thousands of soldiers marched into the square where they set about attacking the demonstrators with sticks and clubs. Two days later, the Politburo, the senior committee of the Communist Party, blamed Deng for the riots, sacked him from all his posts and appointed Hua Guofeng as Vice-Chairman.

Mao had chosen Hua as the man to succeed him. It was a surprising choice as few people knew much about Hua apart from the fact that he was a loyal supporter of Mao. The question people now asked was: would Hua support the Gang of Four after Mao's death? They did not have to wait long for an answer. In September 1976 Mao died and less than a month later Hua made his move.

Crowds fill the square in Beijing to pay their respects to Zhou Enlai

The fall of the Gang of Four

On the night of 6 October 1976, Hua called a special meeting of a small party committee. Two of its four members were Wang Hongwen and Zhang Chunqiao of the Gang of Four. Wang was surprised to find no one there when he arrived at the meeting place. As he turned to leave, security guards appeared from behind a screen and ordered him to put up his hands. When he resisted, he was forced to the ground and handcuffed. The unsuspecting Zhang was arrested when he arrived, while in a nearby room Hua sat watching the events on closed-circuit television. At the same time, security forces moved in quickly to arrest Jiang Qing and her followers.

In this cartoon of the Gang of Four, drawn after they were arrested, Jiang Qing is the central figure sitting in a chair. What are the other three members of the Gang of Four doing? And what is the cartoonist trying to say about the Gang of Four?

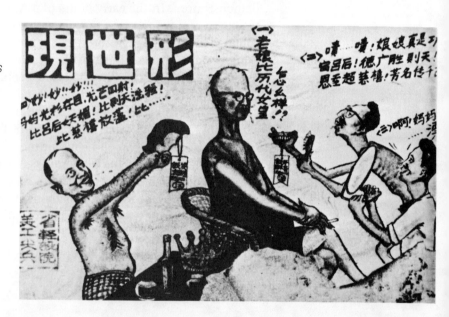

The return of Deng

Hua's decision to seize the Gang of Four and their leading supporters was a popular move, but Hua still lacked enough support to govern China effectively. In the months that followed, Hua came under increasing pressure to bring Deng back to office. When Deng promised in 1977 to be 'a good assistant to Hua', he was given back all his positions in the party. Millions of people took to the streets to celebrate Deng's return. There were carnival processions and firework displays.

Deng, however, had no intention of keeping his word to Hua. In his view, the Cultural Revolution had been a disaster for China and Mao had been responsible for it. He was determined to set China on a new course, but with Hua in control that was impossible. As Deng moved his supporters into key positions in the Communist Party, Hua's power began to slip; in 1981 he was relegated to the position of junior Vice-Chairman.

Tackling the economy

Deng's main concern was to improve and modernise the Chinese economy. Overall much progress had been made since 1949, but many of the machines were old-fashioned and many Chinese factories were inefficient and running at a loss. In addition, the co-operative farms were failing to produce enough food. In 1982 China had to import a record 13.7 million tons of grain to feed its population

Deng had two main answers to these problems. First, China had to learn from other countries. Deng sent students abroad to study engineering and technology. He encouraged foreign companies to set up projects in China in partnership with state-owned Chinese businesses. These projects ranged from textile factories and hotel construction to oil prospecting.

ENERGY AND RAW MATERIAL

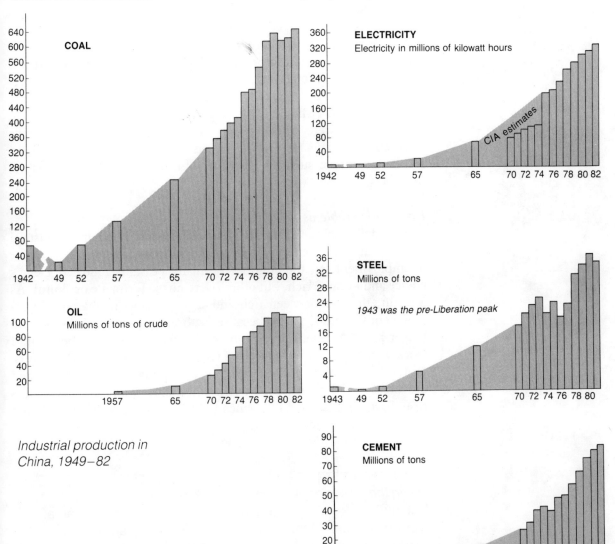

Industrial production in China, 1949–82

Deng's second answer was to provide the Chinese workers with rewards and incentives for hard work. In his view, the Chinese had had their fill of political meetings and slogans calling on them to produce more for the good of the nation. What was the point of working hard if you earned the same as your idle neighbour? What was the point of earning more if there was nothing in the shops that you wanted to buy?

In the countryside, Deng launched an attack on the system of co-operative farming which had been set up in the 1950s. He gave individual peasant families land to farm. Once they had produced a certain amount of grain or rice and handed it over to the State for a fixed price they were free to sell any extra grain they produced at the local market.

In the factories, workers were given bonuses for extra production and they were encouraged to buy shares in their factory. If the factory did well, so did they. Deng told the factory managers to run their factories profitably and to produce what people wanted to buy. It was discovered that in one area there were two million pairs of rubber-soled shoes piled up in warehouses. Nobody was buying them because the style was old-fashioned, yet the factories were still producing them because they were under orders to do so. Now, under Deng's instructions, many factories switched to making goods that would sell in the shops, such as television sets, motor cycles and washing machines.

Economic problems

Deng's new approach ran into some difficulties. Food and industrial production both went up, but so did inflation and the figures for unemployment. In the countryside many peasants followed Deng's advice and became rich, but others were not so fortunate or skilful. As a result, the gap between rich and poor peasants increased. Unemployment increased partly because factories laid off workers they no longer needed in their drive to become efficient. The numbers out of work were swelled by former Red Guards who were allowed to return to the cities. Most lacked skills and training as the schools and universities had been closed down when they were students. Prices rose sharply for the first time since 1949 as the government raised both food prices and factory wages.

Using the evidence: Mao under attack
Despite the problems Deng faced with the economy, he remained a popular figure. Most Chinese saw him as the man who had freed China from the strait-jacket of the Cultural Revolution. Not only had he attacked Mao's policies, but he also went on to attack Mao's reputation as the saviour of China.

A *This photograph was taken in 1981*

Marxist: a follower of Karl Marx, 1818–83, the founder of Communism

B *Chief responsibility for the grave error of the Cultural Revolution does indeed lie with Comrade Mao Zedong ... his prestige reached a peak and he began to get arrogant.... Comrade Mao Zedong was a great Marxist and a great revolutionary. It is true he made gross mistakes during the Cultural Revolution, but his contribution to the Chinese Revolution far outweighs his mistakes.*
The Communist Party's account of its own history, 1981

Questions
1 Describe what you think is happening in source **A**. How does source **B** help you explain why it happened?
2 In what way does the view of Mao expressed in source **B** differ from the view of Mao expressed in China during the Cultural Revolution? (See page 25.)
3 It took eighteen months of discussion before the Communist Party finally agreed on what to say about Mao (source **B**). Why do you think that it took so long and why was the Communist Party determined to write a new account of its own history?

An open society?

After Deng's return to power, China became a much more open society. On television, the Chinese could see the Pope and the American President. They could buy foreign books in translation and they could listen to foreign music. There was more entertainment and fewer political meetings. In their Communist newspapers, the Chinese could read about the darker side of life in China: industrial accidents, crimes and party officials who had used their power for their own ends.

Despite these important changes, the Communist Party continued to keep a tight control over the citizens of China. All Chinese people belong to a unit led by party officials. The unit provides homes and jobs for its members. It hands out ration cards for rice, cloth and soap. If a member of a unit wants to buy an expensive item, such as a sewing machine or a bicycle, he has to apply to the unit for a coupon and he may have to wait a long time before he gets it. If he wants to travel anywhere in China, move to a different job, get married or divorced, he has to get permission from the unit. The unit keeps a record on all its members. Not surprisingly most of the members keep their thoughts to themselves.

Using the evidence: Democracy Wall

For just over a year after Deng's return to office, the Communist Party did allow the Chinese people to express their ideas freely. This had happened only once before; for a brief period in 1957 Mao had encouraged people to criticise the mistakes of the Communist Party. Now, in the big cities, crowds of people gathered to discuss the latest posters pasted up on public walls by individuals who had something they wanted to say. Most of the posters attacked the Cultural Revolution and the Gang of Four, but some went further and criticised Deng's own rule. This period of free speech began and ended on a stretch of wall in front of the bus depot in Beijing. Here, on 'Democracy Wall', as it became known, the first poster went up in November 1978 and the last poster came down in December 1979. Why did the Communist Party shut down Democracy Wall? Why did it change its mind about free speech?

1   *The changing view of the Communist Party*
a)   *[The Chinese people have the right] to speak freely, air their views fully, hold debates and write big character posters.*
                         From the revised Chinese constitution, 1978
b)   *Let the people say what they wish. The heavens will not fall. . . . If a person is to be punished for saying wrong things, no one will say what he thinks.*
                                    People's Daily, January 1979
c)   *All slogans, posters, books, pictures, photographs which oppose the leadership of the Communist Party are prohibited.*
                    Beijing Revolutionary Committee, 28 March 1979
d)   *The Party is the core force leading our cause. A socialist party cannot do without the Party's leadership, there can be*

no doubt about that. . . . If no one listens to the Party committee, if quarrels and bitterness become a daily routine . . . nothing can be done at all.

A leading member of the Communist Party, October 1979

e) *Without the Communist Party, there would have been no new China. . . . Without the leadership of such a Party our country would fall apart.*

Official history of the Communist Party, 1981

2 The views of the poster-writers

f) *The Cultural Revolution must be reassessed. Mao Zedong was 70% good and 30% bad.*

Poster on Democracy Wall, November 1978

g) *The citizens demand freedom of thought and freedom of speech. The system in which a citizen devotes his whole life to a unit where he works must be abolished. Citizens demand the freedom to choose their own jobs, the freedom to express support [for a leader] and freedom of movement.*

Extract from the programme of the China Human Rights Association, founded in January 1979

h) *Do the people support Deng Xiaoping as a person? No, they do not . . . he now wants to strip off his mask as protector of democracy and to crush the democracy movement.*

Wei Jingsheng, a leading campaigner for free speech, 25 March 1979

(Shortly afterwards, he was arrested.)

i) *The Constitution gives the people the right to criticise leaders because they are human beings and not gods. Only through criticism and supervision by the people, can they reduce their errors and avoid being overlords who ride roughshod over the people.*

Wei Jingsheng at his trial in October 1979

3 Time chart of main events

November 1978 First posters go up in Beijing. Wall posters put up in other cities.

January 1979 China Human Rights Association founded.

29 March 1979 Wei Jingsheng arrested. This was followed by the arrest of other leading campaigners for free speech. Posters were only allowed on one site (Democracy Wall).

October 1979 Wei Jingsheng found guilty of working to overthrow the Communist government and sentenced to fifteen years' imprisonment.

December 1979 Beijing street cleaners remove all posters on Democracy Wall. Site closed down.

4 *Photographic evidence*

Photographs a), b) and c) were taken near Democracy Wall between November 1978 and December 1979.

a

b

c

Questions

1 Using sources a) to e), describe how the Communist Party changed its view on free speech between November 1978 and December 1979.

2 What happened between January 1979 and March 1979 to make the Communist Party change its mind and clamp down on free speech?

3a Why did Wei Jingsheng (see source i)) think it was necessary for the Communist Party to allow the people to speak freely and criticise their leaders?

 b What did the leaders of the Communist Party think would happen if they allowed the people to speak freely and criticise their leaders? (See sources d) and e).)

4 Describe what you think is happening in photographs a), b) and c). Write down the order in which you think they were taken and explain your reasons.

5 | CHINA AND THE SUPERPOWERS

China and the outside world

The Chinese are probably more aware of their own history than any other people. Recently, an American was visiting a remote village in the province of Henan where Chinese civilisation began three thousand years ago. In excellent Chinese he asked a group of elderly peasants whether any other foreigner had ever been to the village. 'Yes,' they replied. He asked, 'Was it a Russian in the 1950s?' 'No,' they said. 'Was it a Japanese from the war?' 'No,' they said. 'Was it a Christian missionary at the turn of the century?' 'No.' Finally he gave up. 'It was the Yuan dynasty,' said a man with a white beard. He was referring to the period seven hundred years ago when the Mongols ruled China. 'Some Mongol troops came through the village.'

The Chinese are particularly aware of the hundred years before the Communists came to power. It had been a period of failure and national disaster as the country was taken over by the foreigners. The worst blow came in 1937 when Japan launched a full-scale invasion of China. The Communists were determined to restore China's pride and independence. Mao announced in 1949 that 'the Chinese people will never again be an insulted nation'. Nearly 30 years later Deng Xiaoping agreed with him: 'The Chinese people will never bow and beg and scrape for help.'

According to both Mao and Deng, the real threat to China's independence has come from the United States and the Soviet Union. Since 1945 these two superpowers have competed for influence across the world and one of their main areas of interest has been China. For the first 20 years of Communist rule, the main threat to China appeared to come from the United States. Since 1968–9, the Chinese have become more alarmed about the Soviet Union.

The war in Korea

China's relations with the United States government got off to a bad start with the outbreak of the Korean war in 1950. After Japan had withdrawn from Korea in 1945, the country had been divided at the 38th parallel. In the north there was a Communist government and in the south a government supported by the United States. Attempts to unite the country peacefully had failed. Then on 25 June 1950 an army from North Korea invaded the south.

The Americans were convinced that the invasion had been ordered

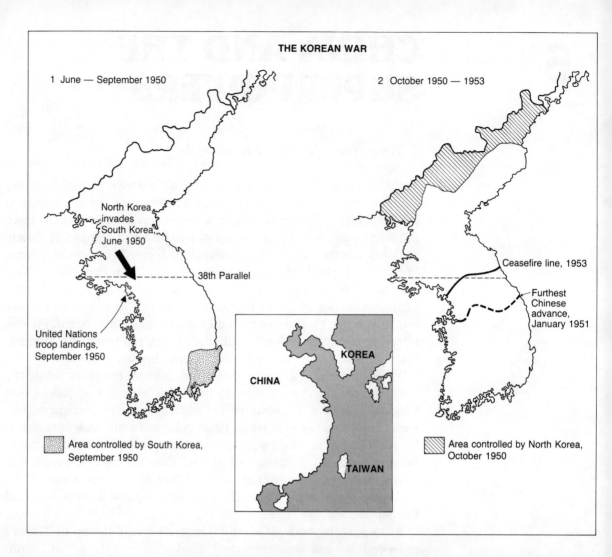

THE KOREAN WAR

1 June — September 1950

North Korea invades South Korea, June 1950

38th Parallel

United Nations troop landings, September 1950

Area controlled by South Korea, September 1950

2 October 1950 — 1953

Ceasefire line, 1953

Furthest Chinese advance, January 1951

Area controlled by North Korea, October 1950

CHINA

KOREA

TAIWAN

by the Soviet Union in agreement with China. They decided to act against this Communist aggression. The US Seventh Fleet was sent to patrol the sea between China and Taiwan to stop the Communists from invading the island. General MacArthur was ordered to drive the North Koreans back across the 38th parallel.

With support from the United Nations, MacArthur drove the Communists back, but he did not stop at the 38th parallel. As his army penetrated deep into North Korea, it became clear that America's war aims had changed. Now they were going to force the Communists out of North Korea.

It was at this point that China entered the war. The Chinese were not prepared to have an American-backed government on its border. The Americans would be tempted to reverse the result of the civil war. They could invade China both from Taiwan and North Korea and then put Chiang Kai-shek back as ruler of China. Zhou Enlai warned the Americans that if their advance continued the Chinese would send in troops.

Chinese troops leaving North Korea. How are the North Koreans reacting to the departure of the Chinese? And why do you think they are behaving in this way?

The Americans took no notice of this warning. As MacArthur's army advanced towards the Chinese border, it was met with a series of massed attacks from a 300 000-strong Chinese army. The Americans withdrew in what became the longest retreat in their history. President Truman considered whether to drop an atom bomb on China and MacArthur urged him to do so. In the end they used the more normal methods of warfare to drive the Communists back. After three years the war ended near to where it had started on the 38th parallel.

The Korean War convinced the United States government that it should take a hard-line attitude towards China. It cut off all trade links and set up military bases in friendly countries near China. It sent troops to Taiwan, promising to defend the island from Communist attack. It made sure that Chiang Kai-shek's government, not Mao Zedong's, represented China at the United Nations.

The war in Vietnam

Shortly after the armistice was signed in Korea in 1953, war broke out in Vietnam. Again American troops became involved and again China felt threatened. After the French pulled out of Vietnam in 1954, the country had become divided like Korea. In the north there was a Communist government and in the south a government backed by the United States. The government in South Vietnam soon came under fierce attack from rebels within the country, who were supported by their allies in North Vietnam.

41

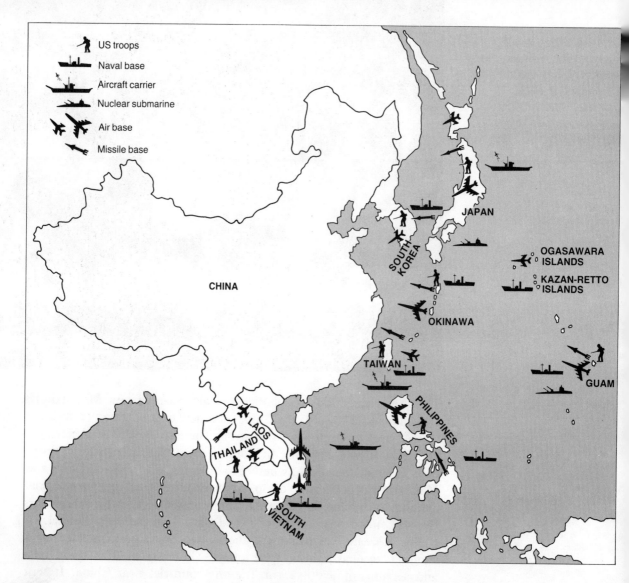

Legend

- US troops
- Naval base
- Aircraft carrier
- Nuclear submarine
- Air base
- Missile base

CHINA

SOUTH KOREA

JAPAN

OGASAWARA ISLANDS

KAZAN-RETTO ISLANDS

OKINAWA

TAIWAN

GUAM

PHILIPPINES

LAOS

THAILAND

SOUTH VIETNAM

The Chinese view of the United States' military threat in 1966

The United States government was determined to prevent South Vietnam from falling to the Communists. It sent in troops to defeat the rebels and in 1965 American aeroplanes started to bomb North Vietnam in order to cut off their supply routes to the south. Bordering onto North Vietnam, China felt threatened by this action. The Chinese stepped up their aid to North Vietnam and warned the United States government that they would send in troops if the Americans invaded North Vietnam.

Despite the presence of half a million troops in South Vietnam and repeated bombing raids on North Vietnam, the United States government was no nearer to winning the war. The country's political leaders were determined not to invade North Vietnam. By 1968 they were beginning to consider how they could withdraw their troops from South Vietnam, and the Chinese realised that the American threat to China was starting to fade.

Vietnam

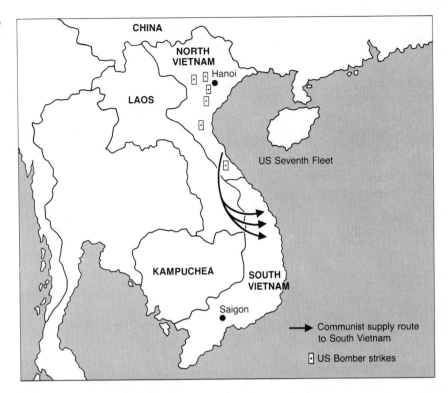

Using the evidence

The American view that China was an aggressive nation determined to spread Communism in Asia goes back to the start of the Korean War when North Korea invaded South Korea. But was Mao Zedong involved in the plans to invade South Korea? Had he discussed it with Stalin when he met him in Moscow six months before the invasion?

A Stalin's treatment of Mao in Moscow in 1949:
   Stalin would sometimes not lay eyes on him [Mao] for days at a time. No one dared to go and see him. Rumours began reaching our ears that Mao was not at all happy, that he was under lock and key and that he was being ignored. When Stalin heard about Mao's complaints, I think he had another dinner for him.
   Nikita Khrushchev: *Khrushchev Remembers*, 1974

B *Nothing seems more certain than that Stalin was the inspirer of the Korean attack and that the orders came from Moscow. It is possible, to be sure, that Mao was told of the move or that he recommended such actions. But in the light of the knowledge that we possess concerning the outright hostility between Stalin and Mao, it seems unlikely that Stalin, secretive as he was, would have outlined his plans to Mao.*

43

If these assumptions are correct (and there will be no way of proving them until Peking and Moscow open many more of their secret files) Moscow emerges as the prime mover in Korea.

Harrison Salisbury:
The Coming War between Russia and China, 1969

C *At that very moment when Dean Acheson, U.S. Secretary of State, announced that South Korea was beyond America's* defence perimeter, *Mao Zedong discussed with Stalin the settlement of Far Eastern affairs and agreed that South Korea should be invaded by the North.*

John Vaizey: *The Lost Peace*, 1983

defence perimeter: the area America was prepared to defend

Questions

1 Which of these sources states or suggests that Mao was involved in the decision to invade South Korea?
2 What two reasons are given in source **B** to support the author's conclusion that Stalin did not consult Mao?
3 Khrushchev's account (source **A**) does not tell us whether or not Stalin consulted Mao about the decision to invade South Korea. Why, then, is it useful to the historian when trying to answer this question?
4 Why, according to source **B**, is it not possible to know for certain whether Mao was involved in the decision to attack South Korea?
5 Which of the following statements do you find most convincing?
    a) North Korea attacked South Korea without the approval of either Stalin or Mao.
    b) Stalin ordered the invasion of South Korea on his own.
    c) Stalin and Mao together ordered the invasion of South Korea.
   Explain your decision and why you have rejected the other two statements.

China and the Soviet Union 1949–69

In 1969 the Soviet Union and China were both pouring in aid to their Communist ally, North Vietnam, in the common fight against American imperialism. At the same time Chinese and Soviet frontier guards were fighting each other at points along their 6 400-kilometre border. Soon both countries had large armies stationed on the border and China was preparing to defend itself against a nuclear attack from the Soviet Union. An American visitor reported that the Chinese were building an underground city in Beijing capable of protecting the entire seven million population from nuclear attack:

> *I saw entrances to these underground tunnels in almost every street and courtyard. The new tunnel network was equipped with electricity, water, food, medical stocks and ventilation systems.*

The two largest Communist countries in the world were preparing for all-out war with each other. Yet in 1950 China and the Soviet Union had signed a Treaty of Friendship; Mao had said that the union of the two countries was 'everlasting and unbreakable'. What had gone wrong? What had broken the Communist partnership?

For much of the past three hundred years, the two countries had been on bad terms. The old tsarist state of Russia had taken full advantage of China's increasing weakness and forced its rulers to hand over about four million square kilometres of territory. Any hopes of a

tsarist: the tsars were the rulers of Russia until they were overthrown in 1917

The Chinese view of border incidents between Chinese and Russian troops in 1969. In both photographs Chinese frontier guards are warning the Russians not to intrude any further

fresh start between the Communist parties of both countries were soon dashed. Stalin had tried to stop the Chinese Communists from winning an outright victory in the civil war. He wanted Mao to rule northern China and Chiang Kai-shek to rule southern China. He thought that the Soviet Union would be more secure with a weak and divided China on its doorstep. When that plan failed and the Communists took over the whole of China, Stalin and his successor, Khrushchev, were determined to keep them under control. They insisted that the Chinese should follow the example of the Soviet Union and accept their leadership.

Mao was not prepared to carry out the orders of the Soviet Union. China was determined to be independent and to work out its own policies. At home, Mao abandoned the Five Year Plan, modelled on the Soviet Union, and launched the Great Leap Forward in 1958. In foreign affairs Mao criticised Khrushchev's view that in the nuclear age Communists could and must live in peace with capitalist countries. Mao argued that countries such as America were out to enslave the rest of the world. Even if the capitalists did start a war, the Communists would eventually win:

> We may lose more than 300 million people. So what. War is war. The years will pass and we'll get to work producing more babies.

Khrushchev was horrified by this view:

> Anyone who thinks that Communism can be advanced by war belongs to the lunatic asylum.

Relations between the two countries went from bad to worse. The 1960s opened with the Soviet withdrawal of all her advisers from China. When the decade ended China was preparing for a nuclear attack from its Communist neighbour.

Using the evidence: China and the bomb
In 1957 the Soviet Union agreed to help China develop the atom bomb. Two years later, Khrushchev refused to carry out the agreement. As a result, relations between the two countries rapidly got worse. Why did Khrushchev make that decision?

A   The Chinese view
The Soviet leaders hold that China should not and must not manufacture nuclear weapons. The Soviet leaders say, how can the Chinese be qualified to manufacture nuclear weapons when they eat watery soup out of a common bowl and do not even have trousers to wear. . . . We will neither crawl to the baton of the Soviet leaders nor kneel before the nuclear blackmail of the U.S. imperialism.
Chinese government publication, 1963

B   The Soviet view
We knew that if we failed to send the bomb to China the Chinese would accuse us of breaking a treaty. On the other hand, they had already begun their smear campaign against us.... We didn't want them to get the idea that we were obedient slaves who would give them whatever they wanted no matter how much they insulted us. We decided to postpone sending them the prototype.

Nikita Khrushchev: *Khrushchev Remembers*, 1974

C   A historian's view
The Sino-Soviet conflict exists and will continue. The Soviet Union possesses nuclear arms; China does not. China has asked Russia for these arms, and Russia has refused to supply them. Why? Because Khrushchev fears that China may use them recklessly and plunge the world into a war of annihilation? Or because, in traditional Russian style, he prefers not to have a strong China up against his own frontier? No doubt for both reasons.

Edward Crankshaw:
The New Cold War: Moscow v Peking, 1965

Sino-Soviet conflict: the dispute between China and the Soviet Union

Questions
1   Summarise the reasons given in each of the three sources to explain why Khrushchev broke the agreement with China.
2   What evidence is there in these extracts that both sides felt that the other side had insulted them?
3   Why do you think the historian's view (source **C**) is different from both the Soviet and Chinese views? Is his view likely to be more or less accurate than the other views? Give reasons for your answer.
4   Using all three sources, write a paragraph explaining your own view on why Khrushchev refused to carry out the agreement.

China and the superpowers since 1969

By 1969 Mao Zedong had become convinced that the Soviet Union had become more of a threat than the United States. While Richard Nixon, the new American President, was starting to withdraw American troops from South Vietnam, the Soviet Union was doubling its troops on the Chinese border. Nixon himself had decided to talk to the Chinese. He wanted all American troops out of South Vietnam without losing the country to the Communists. He hoped that the Chinese would be able to help him, knowing that China did not want a powerful Vietnam, under Soviet influence, on its southern border.

Faced with the Soviet threat, Mao saw the advantages of talking to the Americans. It would force the Soviet Union to shelve any plans it had to attack China. The United States government might be persuaded to drop its out and out support for Chiang Kai-shek in Taiwan, thereby hastening the day when the island would once again become part of mainland China. As a first step towards improved relations, the United States government dropped its objections to Communist China becoming a member of the United Nations. In 1971 the United Nations Assembly voted in favour of Communist China replacing Taiwan as the representative of China.

Communist China's entry into the United Nations was followed in 1972 by President Nixon's visit to China. Millions watched on television as Nixon met the top Chinese leaders and walked along part of the Great Wall of China. Beyond the reach of the cameras, the Chinese secretly agreed to help Nixon in his plan for Vietnam. For its part, the United States government publicly promised to withdraw all its troops from Taiwan 'as the tension in the area diminishes'. Trade restarted between the two countries and cultural and sporting exchanges increased as a result of Nixon's visit. However, China continued to be wary; although American troops were withdrawn from Taiwan, the United States government has continued to supply the island with defensive weapons to protect it from possible Communist attack.

President Nixon meets Chairman Mao

Since 1969, the Chinese have continued to look upon the Soviet Union as the more dangerous of the two superpowers. 'Soviet armed forces,' they stated in 1982, 'threaten China from the north, the west and the south.' In the north, the Soviet Union had set up military bases in Mongolia, a short distance from Beijing. In the west, the Soviet Union invaded and occupied Afghanistan, on China's border, in 1979. In the south, Vietnam, firmly allied to the Soviet Union, has become the most powerful state in the area. Vietnam became a united country under the control of the Communists in 1975, two years after the American troops were withdrawn from South Vietnam. In 1978, the Vietnamese invaded and occupied the neighbouring state of Kampuchea. The following year the Chinese struck back by sending an army across the border into Vietnam. They captured and destroyed three provincial capitals and then withdrew after suffering at least 20 000 casualties.

Is China a superpower?

The Chinese view the superpowers as a threat both to China and to world peace. Deng Xiaoping remarked in 1974:

> *The two superpowers are the sources of a new world war. They carry on a heavily contested arms race, station massive forces abroad and set up military bases everywhere.*

Since 1949, the Chinese have dealt successfully with the superpowers. China has kept its independence from both the United States and the Soviet Union. Through its own efforts China has developed nuclear weapons and the country has one of the two largest armies in the world. China's very success raises an important question. Has the nation become the world's third superpower? Has China the power and the desire to compete with the United States and the Soviet Union for influence across the world?

Using the evidence

A   The Chinese view
The superpowers want to be superior to others and lord it over the others. At no time, neither today nor ever in the future will China be a superpower, subjecting others to its aggression, interference or bullying.
    Communist China's delegate at the United Nations, 1971

B   Foreign views
(i)   *Is Communist China basically aggressive? Since 1949, she has given armed support to North Korea, invaded areas claimed by India, annexed Tibet and supplied weapons to*

annexed: taken over by force

49

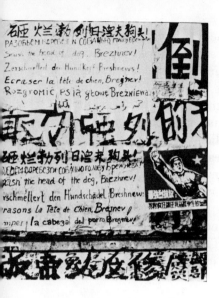

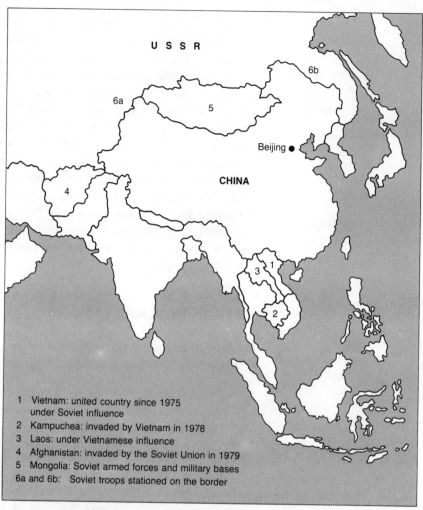

Above: *in this anti-Soviet poster, Brezhnev, the Soviet leader, is attacked in several languages*
Right: *the Chinese view of the Soviet threat*

1 Vietnam: united country since 1975
   under Soviet influence
2 Kampuchea: invaded by Vietnam in 1978
3 Laos: under Vietnamese influence
4 Afghanistan: invaded by the Soviet Union in 1979
5 Mongolia: Soviet armed forces and military bases
6a and 6b: Soviet troops stationed on the border

India. In defence of her actions China would argue that she was coming to the aid of friendly neighbours and in the other instances she was ... [taking back] ... control over areas which had traditionally formed part of her national territory. She has never attempted to conquer the weaker states that surround her ... nor does she have any troops stationed on foreign soil.

Richard Tames: *China Today*, 1975

(ii)   Despite having a 4.5 million-man army, nuclear weapons and inter-continental ballistic missiles, China is not a superpower. Peking's ability to affect international events is limited. The weapons of China's army, navy and airforces are largely antiquated versions of thirty-year-old Soviet designs. China's strategic doctrine calls for defence by a people's war rather than any aggressive strike outside the country's borders.

Fox Butterfield: *China*, 1982

C   Comparative figures on military spending 1977−82
    (in millions of dollars):

	1977	1978	1979	1980	1981	1982
U.S.A.	137	138	139	144	154	170
Soviet Union	126	128	130	131	134	135
China	33	37	49	43	37	39

D   Size of population and armed forces 1983:

	Population	Total Armed Forces
U.S.A.	234 516 000	2 136 400
Soviet Union	271 800 000	5 050 000
China	1 008 175 300	4 100 000

E   Timechart

1950	Chinese troops take over Tibet
1950	Chinese troops invade North Korea
1962	Border clashes with India over disputed territory
1964	China tests first atom bomb
1967	China tests first hydrogen bomb
1969	Border clashes with the Soviet Union
1979	Chinese troops invade North Vietnam

Questions

1   Look carefully at document C. Pick out two ways in which the pattern of military spending in China is different from that of both the United States and the Soviet Union. Suggest possible reasons for these differences.

2   Use sources B(ii) and D to suggest two reasons why China has such a large army. Does the fact that China has the second largest army in the world prove that it has become a superpower? Give reasons for your answer.

3   Write the speech that the Chinese delegate might make at the United Nations in the 1980s on the theme of China and the superpowers. In your speech explain what China thinks of the superpowers, using examples of both Soviet and American aggression towards China since 1949. You should also refer to sources B(i) and (ii) to support your argument that China is not a superpower.

CHANGE IN COMMUNIST CHINA

The Communist achievement

China's history as a nation goes back three thousand years. The Communists have been in power for less than 40 years, yet during this short period they have probably done more to change China than any of its previous rulers. The country has become one of the world's leading industrial producers. It has successfully defended itself from the threat of invasion and its voice in world affairs is listened to with respect. Nobody, any more, looks upon China as 'the sick man of Asia'.

The Communists have improved people's living standards despite the Great Leap Forward and the Cultural Revolution. In 1949 the average age of death in China was 32; in the 1980s it has doubled to 64. Signs of improvement are most obvious in the cities. One observer noted in 1981:

All around me I could see evidence to confirm the official claims....
On the streets of Beijing young adults towered above their grand-parents and virtually all the children attended secondary as well as primary schools. Before 1949 there had been unhealthy slums in the city. These had all gone.

Using machines to harvest the rice

In the countryside, where the land is flat and fertile the peasants have prospered. When William Hinton returned to Longbow (see chapter 1) in the 1970s, he found that the growing village now had a cement works and saw-mill which provided most of the village's income. The peasants were producing far more food per acre than in the past as a result of using chemical fertilisers and machines to plant and harvest the crops. Each child went to school for eight years, each family received medical care for a small charge and each person had a free bath once a week.

Poverty remains

However, many of China's 750 million peasants are still very poor. In the more remote, less fertile areas peasants continue to live in mud huts with a few pieces of furniture made out of pounded earth and an inadequate diet that consists of rice or hard buns together with a few vegetables and sweet potatoes. Most peasants still use the old methods of farming, as Fox Butterfield described in 1982:

night soil: human and animal excrement used to fertilise the soil

> *Young peasants, their backs hunched under swaying bamboo shoulder poles with buckets at each end, were walking along the narrow mud dikes between the paddies carrying loads of night soil. Then they waded barefoot into the unplanted fields and upturned their buckets of slop ... other peasants bent double at the waist, were moving backwards step by step as they transplanted the seedlings.... During a full day's drive I saw only a handful of tractors ... ploughing was still the work of men hitched to lumbering water buffaloes.*

Transplanting rice by hand

The population problem

The main reason why so many people are still poor is the rapid increase in population that has taken place since 1949. Although the Chinese peasants produce twice as much food as they did when the Communists came to power, there are twice as many mouths to feed. In the space of 30 years, the population of China has doubled from 500 million to one billion, which is roughly one quarter of the world's total population. Since the late 1970s the government has introduced drastic measures to slow down the population increase. It has strongly encouraged families to have only one child whereas three has been the average. Every couple who promise to have only one child receive a 'planned parenthood glory coupon' which gives them a five per cent bonus on what they earn, plus extra grain rations and free medical care for their child. If they have a second child, they have to pay all the benefits back; if they have a third, they have to pay a fine of between five and ten per cent of their earnings. The campaign has been effective in the cities, but less successful in the countryside where peasants want several children to increase the family's income and to look after them when they are old. Peasants, unlike factory workers, do not receive a pension when they give up work. In addition, many peasants still want a son in the family, despite all the efforts that the government has made to achieve equality between the sexes. The following extract illustrates the real difficulties the Communists face in attempting to change attitudes and habits that have been handed down from generation to generation across the centuries of China's long history.

Government poster proclaiming that 'One child is enough'

Using the evidence: the slaughter of baby girls

Chinese peasants are allowing their baby girls to die at such a rate that a call has gone out to save them. Nothing but murder or deliberate neglect can explain why in some communes just 200 girls survive out of every 500 children born, although China's census shows that the number of girl babies at birth is only marginally less than boys.

These figures, reported in China Youth Daily, *highlight the resurgence of female infanticide, usually by abandonment or 'exposure' but sometimes by drowning. . . . The rise in the killing of girls is a direct result of China's one-child family drive which seeks dramatically to reduce the population of more than one billion.*

Early this year a Central Committee member admitted that women are still cursed and beaten by their husbands and mothers-in-law for bearing girl babies. Drowning girl babies often occurs, he said.

Many Chinese still believe that without a son there can be no descendants. Only male children hand down the family name and can worship and nourish their ancestors.

Jonathan Mirsky: *The Observer*, 1982

Questions

1 According to this article, what methods are some Chinese peasants using to kill their baby daughters?
2 Explain how *China Youth Daily* came to the conclusion that in some communes large numbers of baby girls were being killed.
3 Explain fully why, according to this article, there has been a rise in the killing of baby girls recently.
4 What reason does the author put forward to explain why sons are more important than daughters to many Chinese? What other reason can you think of to explain this belief?
5 How do you think the Chinese government should tackle this problem? Suggest what they might do to stop the slaughter of baby girls while continuing to try and stop the population increase.

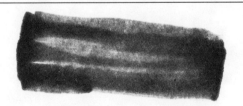

INDEX